Wow, That's Woolly!

CAMELS

Gareth Stevens
PUBLISHING

Beth Gottlieb

Please visit our website, www.garethstevens.com. For a free color catalog of all our high-quality books, call toll free 1-800-542-2595 or fax 1-877-542-2596.

Cataloging-in-Publication Data
Names: Gottlieb, Beth.
Title: Camels / Beth Gottlieb.
Description: New York : Gareth Stevens Publishing, 2023. | Series: Wow, that's woolly! | Includes glossary and index.
Identifiers: ISBN 9781538279397 (pbk.) | ISBN 9781538279410 (library bound) | ISBN 9781538279403 (6pack) | ISBN 9781538279427 (ebook)
Subjects: LCSH: Camels--Juvenile literature.
Classification: LCC QL737.U54 G68 2023 | DDC 591.4--dc23

Published in 2023 by
Gareth Stevens Publishing
29 E. 21st Street
New York, NY 10010

Designer: Olivia Lo Sardo
Editor: Kristen Nelson

Portions of this work were originally authored by Cleo Bloom and published as *Camels*. All new material this edition authored by Beth Gottlieb.

Photo credits: Cover AnanKaewkhammul/Shutterstock.com; camel art IvanaKontic/Shutterstock.com; p. 4 aleksander hunta/Shutterstock.com; p. 5 HappyOwl/Shutterstock.com; p. 6 DavidSteele/Shutterstock.com; p. 7 Valerii_M/Shutterstock.com; p. 8 simoly/Shutterstock.com; p. 9 georgemal33/Shutterstock.com; p. 11 MatyasRehak/Shutterstock.com; p. 13 SubAtomicScope/Shutterstock.com; p. 15 Poznyakov/Shutterstock.com; p. 17 salarko/Shutterstock.com; p. 18 al7/Shutterstock.com; p. 19 J.Natayo/Shutterstock.com; p. 21 NataliaFrenta/Shutterstock.com

Printed in the United States of America

CPSIA compliance information: Batch #CSGS23: For further information, contact Gareth Stevens, New York, New York, at 1-800-542-2595.

CONTENTS

Words in the glossary appear in **bold** type the first time they are used in the text.

WHAT'S WOOL?

Wool is any **fiber** produced by animals that is collected and used to make cloth. More animals produce wool than you think, including llamas, alpacas, and of course, sheep. One is a well-known desert **dweller** that carries its own water on a long journey: the camel! Camel hair has been used by people for thousands of years.

Today, camel hair is used to make goods all over the world. Its lovely brown color and warmth make it a highly valued wool.

PULL BACK THE WOOL

In the past, in parts of Africa, owning many camels meant you had wealth.

Camel wool is about as strong as sheep's wool.

CAMEL KINDS

Camels can have one hump or two. By counting how many humps a camel has, you can tell what kind it is. Arabian camels, also called dromedaries, have one hump on their back. All Arabian camels are **domesticated** today.

Bactrian camels have two humps. There are two kinds of Bactrian camels: domesticated and wild. Wild Bactrian camels are considered a critically endangered species. That means they are at a very high risk of dying out completely. There are only about 1,500 wild Bactrian camels left.

PULL BACK THE WOOL

Camels' humps store fat.

Arabian camel

Camels use the fat in their hump for energy. It can be turned into water too!

THE CAMEL LOOK

Adult camels are about 7 feet (2.1 m) tall at the hump. Arabian camels weigh up to 1,600 pounds (725 kg), and Bactrian camels weigh up to 1,800 pounds (815 kg).

Camels are covered in hair that is commonly light brown. They have a long neck and a small head. Their long legs end in feet with two big toes. Camels have large eyes **protected** by hairy eyebrows and two rows of long eyelashes. Their upper lip is rough and split into two parts.

PULL BACK THE WOOL

Camels have special noses that can close to block out sand.

CAMEL ADAPTATIONS

Many of camels' features are **adaptations** that help them live in the desert.

DESERT LIFE

Camels are native to deserts. Arabian camels live in northern Africa and southwestern Asia. Domesticated Bactrian camels live in central and east Asia. Wild Bactrian camels live in the Gobi Desert in Mongolia and China. Some camels now also live in Australia.

Thanks to the stored fat in their humps, camels can travel up to 100 miles (160 km) in the desert without water. When they do come across water, they can drink up to 30 gallons (115 L) in just 13 minutes!

PULL BACK THE WOOL

Camels almost never sweat! Their bodies hold on to as much water as possible.

Camels are herbivores, which means they eat only plants. Camels can survive on the water from plants alone for several weeks during the winter.

IN THE GROUP

Camels are **mammals**. In the wild, groups are made up of many females and one male. A group of camels is called a caravan or a herd.

Camel mothers give birth to one baby at a time. Baby camels are called calves. They're born without humps. They're born with their eyes open and can run the same day they're born. Calves stay with their mothers for several years. Camels reach adulthood when they're about five years old. They can live for up to 50 years.

PULL BACK THE WOOL

In the wild, some herds have only male camels. These are called bachelor herds.

Mother camels and babies hum to one another!

CAMELS AND PEOPLE

Camels have been working with people for thousands of years! More than 3,000 years ago, people living throughout the grasslands and deserts of Africa and Asia domesticated camels. Since that time, people have kept them as livestock. People ride camels, use them to carry heavy loads, eat their meat, and drink their milk.

One of the main uses of domesticated camels is as **transportation**. An adult male camel can carry 440 pounds (200 kg) on its back for a short period of time.

PULL BACK THE WOOL

In short bursts, camels can run at speeds up to 40 miles (65 km) per hour.

Female camels can produce up to 6 quarts (5.7 L) of milk per day.

COLLECTING THE COAT

Camels have beautiful, thick coats of golden-brown hair. People have long used this hair to make warm clothes that last a long time.

Camels have an outer coat of coarse hair and an undercoat of soft hair. The undercoat is collected and made into cloth. Camels **shed** their hair naturally during the late spring and early summer. It's during this time that the hair is collected. Since the outer coat and undercoat shed at the same time, people use combs to sort the hairs.

PULL BACK THE WOOL

One camel can produce 17.5 to 22 pounds (8 to 10 kg) of hair per year.

Bactrian camel hair is most often used to make camel hair goods.

WEAVING WOOL

Before it can be made into cloth, sorted camel hair needs to be washed well. Any dirt present is removed. The sorted and washed hair then goes through a process called dehairing. During dehairing, more coarse hairs are removed, leaving behind only the softest pieces. Only about 30 percent of this hair is judged good enough for fabric making.

Next, the hair can be spun into yarn. The process by which yarn is made into cloth is called weaving.

PULL BACK THE WOOL

Today, China is the leading producer of camel hair products.

The camel's soft undercoat is what is commonly used for clothing. The coarser outer hairs are used in other ways.

COOL CAMELS

Camels may be seen as working animals, but the goods made from their wool can cost a lot of money. They are known to be high **quality** and last a long time. Today, camel hair is used to make jackets, skirts, gloves, hats, scarves, and more!

Camels have worked alongside people for thousands of years. Their many uses are still important today! From transportation and carrying loads to producing beautiful wool, camels are hardworking animals.

Camel hair cloth has often been part of very **fashionable** companies' clothing.

GLOSSARY

adaptation: A change in a type of animal that makes it better able to live in its surroundings.

domesticated: Bred and raised for use by people.

dweller: Someone that lives in a place.

fashionable: Currently popular.

fiber: A thin thread of natural or human-made material that can be used to make cloth.

mammal: A warm-blooded animal that has a backbone and hair, breathes air, and feeds milk to its young.

protect: To keep safe.

quality: The standard or grade of something.

shed: To lose fur.

transportation: The act of moving people or things from one place to another.

FOR MORE INFORMATION

Books

Reed, Ellis M. *Llamas and Alpacas.* Mankato, MN: The Child's World, 2020.

Riggs, Kate. *Camels.* Mankato, MN: The Creative Company, 2023.

Websites

Easy Science for Kids: Camels—The Big and Awkward Desert Animals

easyscienceforkids.com/all-about-camels/

Read more about camels and other animals.

National Geographic for Kids: Bactrian Camel

kids.nationalgeographic.com/animals/mammals/facts/bactrian-camel

Find out more about one kind of camel.

Publisher's note to educators and parents: Our editors have carefully reviewed these websites to ensure that they are suitable for students. Many websites change frequently, however, and we cannot guarantee that a site's future contents will continue to meet our high standards of quality and educational value. Be advised that students should be closely supervised whenever they access the internet.

INDEX